DIASPORA

ECHOES FROM ASMARA

ELSA HAILEMARIAM

Copyright © 2022

Elsa Hailemariam

ISBN
978-1-958400-23-4

All Rights Reserved. Any unauthorized reprint or use of this material is strictly prohibited. No part of this book may be reproduced or transmitted in any form or by any means, electronic or mechanical, including photocopying, recording, or by any information storage and retrieval system without express written permission from the author.

All reasonable attempts have been made to verify the accuracy of the information provided in this publication. Nevertheless, the author assumes no responsibility for any errors and/or omissions.

Contents

Dedication 4

Acknowledgments 5

Chapter 01 | Growing up 1

Chapter 02 | Life Changes 10

Chapter 03 | Leaving Asmara behind 16

Chapter 04 | A new home 25

Chapter 05 | Struggles 30

Chapter 06 | Lessons 38

Chapter 07 | Chaos in asmara 44

Chapter 08 | Family 61

Chapter 09 | Reunion 70

Chapter 10 | Memories 72

DEDICATION

Father his wisdom and humanity Mother her endurance pillars of our family. Am so blessed to be their daughter.

ACKNOWLEDGEMENTS

I thank God for all the Blessing in my life. Explicitly my two sons Merih Gebremedhin and Medhane Teclay. My two grandchildren Layla and Dhalia who flourish my life daily. My daughter in law Lula Lul Bahri (the pearls of the sea) Thank you.

Merih your patience and resilience which I have learned a lot and Medhane your enthusiasm and friendship. Thank you both for bearing with me.

Salome and Miriam Kidane, my nieces thank you for all the love and being there for me. Salome and David thank you for my grandniece, Hellina, who is energy to our life. Hannah and Thomas Hagos, my niece and nephew, who have been there for me, thank you for your love. Gelila Mulugeta my niece your Motto of entrepreneur is quite a lesson to earn.

All my eight siblings with all your children and extended family and all my cousins, who are part of the journey in my life I cannot thank you enough.

Especial thanks for my brother, Yamane Hailemarim who joined the EPLF at his tender age and fought made it to Eritrean Independence May 24, 1991. Still serving his country which I am proud of and great full for his constant advice.

To all people I met at Diaspora and who helped me in shaping my life as a straggling new mother. In particular my friend over 45 years Jenifer Leander, who was there for me and still is my best friend thank you Jenifer. My good friend and comrade Daughter Sophia Tesfamariam, I thank you for all the motivation that you gave me. My young friend Enesta Jones for all your support and to adopted me as mom I am so great full to have you. Last but not least, my childhood friend Brihti Keshi Maasho and her husband Brhanre Asgodom (Salvatore) who were and are still by my side and helped me in shaping my life at Diaspora's great full of having as my friends. The Eritrean youth at Diaspora especially YPFDJ, who inspired me to Wright a book in the English luggage.

CHAPTER 01 | GROWING UP

"Childhood means simplicity. Look at the world with the child's eye - it is very beautiful."

-Kailash Satyarthi.

I remember Asmara that I saw with the eyes of an innocent, a child. Perhaps, it is the reason that no place is more beautiful for me than my beloved Asmara, my hometown on the highlands of Eritrea. Even to this day, nothing and no place is equivalent to Asmara, and the blissful years I spent there.

I remember a young girl, adorned in a loose-cut colorful dress with ringing bracelets, running around the verandah, rushing to grab the first bite of my mother's *zigni*. I recall how Aboy always wanted everyone to eat together, traditionally meal is served in a short round table woven with straws (GriChat) surrounded by stools, and mother, strict as she was, would hide her annoyance at the girl's mischief. Nevertheless, she was well aware and proud of the effect her cooking had on people.

My favorite time was the end of school year closing. It's the raining season. Mostly it rained during lunch time when almost everyone is home for lunch. Rain would stop and adults are off to work. Asmara streets so clean and the crispy air all students on school break, flood the streets of Asmara. Boys are gathering at the tea shops and girls would be visiting each one house taking turn, just walking through the beautiful streets and building of Asmara and chatting about school year about classmates and sharing jokes was a wonderful pass time I miss.

That's how my story began. Life was simple at home. Born in beloved Asmara, the capital and glory of Eritrea, during the reign of Haile Selassie.

Growing up among music, neighbors, laughter, and childhood bliss makes you one of the most fortunate people in the world—spending my days visiting relatives, running around the hills, and exploring cinemas, the marketplace with a display of fresh fruits and vegetable in the city and the farmers flowing with their product to sell products. Going to Massawa, for swimming on pristine beach of the Red Sea enjoying the blue sky and water and hot sand walking by. The interaction was so much to miss.

The buzz of youth never gave me the time to acknowledge the colonial influence over Eritrea's city Asmara, that I was deeply rooted into the harmonious life between the two main religions, Christians and Muslims.

Our daily interaction street walk and traditional clothing and sharing our daily events at school and home, there was nothing to concern or worries for young girl so much of shield from both the Muslim and Christian cultured community. Asmara was my world, the origin of my being. The story cannot go further without describing my hometown.

My grandparents were natives, farmers by profession. They lived a harmonious country life. Therefore, I am one of those fortunate individuals who enjoyed the unscathed life of countryside as well, even though I was a city girl.

Visiting the countryside on winter (its summer here the months from the end of June till the end of August) was a special treat, we will go to see the farmer plowing the land with a pair of oxen and watching herds of sheep and goats on the hill side and all the cows and oxen, shepherds caring for all their herds, it was unforgettable event I use to enjoy.

More than 75% of the Eritrean population lives in rural areas. My father and his father and forefathers were the part of that population. It gave me the opportunity to visit my ancestral home in the village many times.

I loved spending time looking after the herds of farm animals with my father whenever I was taken to the countryside. I remember the annual children festival, autumn the harvest season, Hoye! Hoye! When children went singing from one house to another, receiving the treats of roasted chickpeas. In my memory, I miss my father's village as much as I miss Asmara.

Eritrea being the Italian colony and the land of prosperity of the Italians. For native Eritreans especially for youth living in the farms of the countryside, both from the high lands and lowlands it was a dream to come through.

However, Asmara was not built to entertain Eritreans. The natives were not even allowed to enter the city, with the exception of labor force. The Italians built the city primarily for themselves, making it like a typical Italian town, from architecture to its own car race (the event called, Asmara circuit).

Asmara used to be a small village on the high lands when Italy occupied it in 1889. The town started to grow rapidly under Italian supervision. The real history of Asmara goes back to 800 BCE. The legend says that four clans used to live in the area of the Kebessa Plateau (highland). They were frequently attacked by clans living in the low land. The four women of each clan united to defeat their enemies and decided to join against them, and the men agreed.

What happened to the clans and their attack is debated but relatively remains unknown; but since then, the village was named Arbate Asmera

(Arbatien Sesmera), which in the Tigrinya language means "the four" (in feminine plural) who united them. Eventually, the term Arbate was dropped to use only Asmara, which means [feminine plural, referring to the women] united them." Italians changed the name to their version, Asmara, when they conquered the land. The majority of non-Eritreans use this westernized version Asmara.

As for the aesthetics, the capital city adopted an Italian architectural look. Europeans experimented on Asmara with radical new designs. The Italian colonist structures turned out so well that in the 1930s, Asmara began to be called Picola Italia (Roma), the Little Rome.

UNESCO (United Nations Educational, Scientific and Cultural Organization) made Asmara a World Heritage Site in July 2017, saying, "It is an exceptional example of early modernist urbanism at the beginning of the 20th century and its application in an African context." Asmara was made the capital city under Italian rule in the last years of the 19th century and thus, heavily remained under colonial influence.

The city looked like Roma. Asmara was called "Picola Roma" (the little Roma). Nowadays, most of the buildings of Asmara have an Italian origin. Some shops are still named in Italian.

The three main architectural styles you will find in Asmara are the art deco style, the Victorian style, and the Italian new roman style. The Cinema Impero is a famous art deco building of Asmara. As famous as well, there is the Pension Africa, a cubist building. The Europeans at that time used to say that Asmara was a place to experiment "new radical designs". Some buildings are neo-Romanesque, such as the Roman Catholic Cathedral, some villas are built in a late Victorian style. Art Deco influences are found throughout the city. Architects were restricted ,by nothing.

There are a lot of religious sites in the town of Asmara. Such as the catholic cathedral, the eclectic cathedral, mosques, and the Coptic Enda Mariam cathedral which is one of the most impressive buildings of Asmara. Colored wall pictures done by contemporary artists can be seen in different parts of the town. The town also has traditional markets. It has little shops. The inhabitants are reputed warm and open people.

Eritrean cuisine is a reflection of the country's history. The *Injerra* is commonly eaten in the rural areas. It is pancake-like bread that is usually eaten together with a sauce called *Tsebhi*. The sauce mostly contains a hot and spicy meat variety, but sometimes a vegetable dish (*Alicha*)is also used as a base. In the urban centers, one finds the strong influence of Italian cuisine, and pasta is served in all restaurants.

The lowland groups have a different food tradition than the highlands with the staple food being goat's meat, porridge (*Asida* in Arabic) made of sorghum and served with yogurt or cottage cheese.

Food Customs are different at Ceremonial Occasions. Both Islam and the Orthodox Christian tradition require rigorous observance of fasts and food taboos. Several periods of fasting, the longest being Lent among the Orthodox and Ramadan among Muslims, have to be adhered to by all adults. During religious celebrations, however, food and beverages are served in plenty. Usually an ox, sheep, or goat is slaughtered. The meat and the intestines and liver (Dulet) are served together with the *Injerra*. Traditional beer (*SWA*) from sergume used for Christians and ABAKE (Fenue Greek) for Muslims is brewed in the villages and is always served during ceremonial occasions.

Women in Asmara, Eritrea are known for their vibrant dressing. The significant clothing includes JEDID made from a white cotton in various styles, *Zuria*a and *Chiffon* that represents the culture of the city. The dress is said to be one that Eritrean women often wore during wedding ceremonies.

A *Zuria* is a dress which is paired with a big scarf and Tilfi with detailed designs, mostly hand woven. Tigrinya women in Eritrea enthusiastically wear them. Traditional *Zurias* go to the ankles, with a gauze hood around the head and shoulders. Lowland women dress differently in colorful cotton with variety design They pair it with matching colorful jewelry.

The rich culture, history, and beauty of Asmara can mesmerize anyone. Eritrea was visited by Europeans, and Americans, and neighboring countries, Arabs, Yemenis and Sudanese. Mostly the Sudanese newlywed use to make their honeymoon trips in Asmara and Masawa to enjoy the beautiful beaches of the Sea. It must boggle your mind how someone can think of fleeing from my beautiful hometown. Destiny, I did.

Immigrants! People who leave their homeland, their culture, their loved ones, chasing big dreams. Making a home in a strange country alters their fate. The United States, where people believe piles of treasure await everyone. Dreamers from all over the globe migrate to American lands to claim their stake in this treasure. Some succeed in taking root in the kingdom of riches. While some fade away in the crowd, victims of a cultural shock and homesickness, never to be found. There are great stories of joy and sorrow among immigrants.

I, Senbet, have another of those stories to tell. I, who at the age of seventeen, landed in America, confused yet ambitious, uncertain but resolved, alone but hopeful. This is how it began.

CHAPTER 02 | LIFE CHANGES

Dreams can never be achieved if not acted upon. You have to take actions and change things that are hurdle in the way of making your dream reality. In my family, my father was a sensitive dreamer. I took after him in nurturing dreams and taking enthusiastic action to fulfill them.

My father (Aboy) was always different among the crowd of conservatives. He nurtured out-of-the-box thoughts when everyone was happy to farm in his hometown. While everyone realized the necessity of education decades later, Aboy craved and encouraged higher education from the beginning.

With his revolutionary beliefs, high ambitions, and big dreams to make something of his life, he left the countryside at the tender age of twelve.

Aboy knew nothing, had nothing planned. The only thing that he was aware of was his desire to learn and adapt. He left his home with the dream of establishing roots in Asmara's business world. So, with minimal education and no assets, he started his own business of delivering goods.

However, a different approach to everything was reflected in his work too, since the beginning. Means his way of doing business was always innovative instead of the traditional old methods.

His business model at that time was similar to what we know as drop-shipping today. At that time, nearly no one knew that we could make commission money by delivering goods to the customers' door. That was how Aboy was then.

I sometimes wonder how different things would have been if Aboy could have the higher education he desired or the resources of the modern world like seemingly unlimited benefits of information technology and easy access to computers and other gadgets.

The same goes for my mother. Undoubtedly, she would have been a famous chef with the exposure she could get through social media and kitchen appliances she could never use. Her *Zigni* would have been recognized by all. But at that time, these things were non-existent. Nevertheless, my father proceeded on his dream and opened his own store (grocery) and storage of recycled used bottles. But the prospects of career and financials never dampened their spirits, happiness, and love for each other.

Aboy always said that although they achieved what they wanted to in the business world by becoming the owner of their entrepreneurial efforts, they found the most significant asset in the form of each other's love and companionship, which was triple folded with the birth of each child.

As a result, my parents lovingly produced and raised nine children, giving utmost love to each of us, thus building an aura of confidence and self-worth—a stark contrast to most other children of the time. In particular, female offspring in most Asmara families and other eastern regions were severely discriminated against. Culturally women were looked at as domestic management, having children and looking after their welfare.

So, Aboy could not do much to quench his thirst for success, but his quick business setup after arriving in Asmara gave him a good start in the city. He established his business and married my mother at an early age.

Mother did not only become his partner in life but his business too. We were raised by a loving couple who were partners to each other in every sense. There was nothing that could tarnish our upbringing and childhood in Asmara.

I would be eternally grateful to my parents for the confidence, trust, and freedom they gave us. Although the culture hindered many things that Aboy wanted us to achieve, I still consider myself fortunate as my youth was far better than many others.

In Asmara, the day began with echoes of Azan (Muslims' call to prayer), which was soon followed by the massive bells of the Catholic Cathedral chime when the Orthodox Church celebrates its early morning mass.

The two religions lived in Asmara, like the hands in gloves. We spent our days in the harmonious bliss of their mixed culture. We were adaptable like our hometown. Asmara adapted to the Italians and then to American culture. I did not see the time when Italian culture took root in the city but witnessed the rise of American influence to its fullest.

My childhood was marked by the American fever, which took over the world with a craze. Soon Asmara also came into the grips of this fever. The Bazooka bubblegum and blue jeans became the lifestyle norms in the city.

The US military (Kagnew Station) base in Asmara and Peace Corp teachers at high schools played a significant role in adapting things from the Western culture. People, especially youth, were incredibly impressed with their aura of freedom and high headedness. I was influenced, too. Maybe a notch more than the other Asmara kids of my age.

I began to develop profound aspirations to become progressive and independent. I explored and deluded into the deep ocean of realizations that only to go abroad and study could make me a part of civilization, then. Wherever I went, whoever I talked to, led me to one conclusion that only higher education can help me achieve my dreams. I was lucky that Aboy was always supportive of higher education, but even he couldn't do anything in the face of our culture and tradition at the time.

The eastern world has not evolved to accept women as an equally important entity of society. The female population has gained their freedom, in many aspects, in the western side of the globe, but things were entirely different in countries like Eritrea.

Regardless of the exotic beauty and their history of uniting their people for their land e.g. (Arbate Asmera) Eritrean women are famous for; they were very much domesticated by men to breed, and care for the household and children.

Although raising a family is the greatest and most challenging job that requires knowledge and educated consciousness, people did not think along these lines back in the 1960s and 1970s. Girls were raised with the sole objective of getting married and making homes.

However, fortunately, now Eritrea is an independent country, trying to match its pace with the world. Therefore, Eritrean women are now liberal to be educated and join the working force of economy, side by side with men.

Coming back to my time in Asmara, I would say that Stability is the Motor of Destination, yet we humans take the chance to plan our destination.

I did the same. I chose Eyob to be my life partner. Soon I had to share my decision with Aboy. He took full responsibility and started the protocol of the wedding. Traditionally it is much harder to give away a daughter than to have a son marrying and bringing a bride.

I was about to step into the whole new world of married life. This was as difficult for my parents as it was for me. But I had to move towards my dream, and in my mind, I was doing that, not knowing that what would the future bring and how would my life change.

CHAPTER 03 | LEAVING ASMARA BEHIND

Where we love is home, home that our feet may leave, but not our hearts.

Oliver Wendell Holmes, Sr.

I only wish I didn't have to leave home to make my dreams real. But there was no other way. I always placated my heart thinking that I might leave my home physically, but my essence will remain here. My soul will always belong to Asmara and my home. So, I welcomed Eyob in my life with no qualms and an open hopeful heart.

Eyob, my husband, was a God sent for me and my dreams. If it had not been for him, my dreams would have remained just that, dreams. Aboy and I were doing everything to pull my dreams off the ground. I worked very hard to earn good grades in high school.

I was doing well to achieve good grades in school, and my mind was all set to get into a good college.

I knew Aboy would support me in every way he could. But also, I didn't want him to be looked down on for going against the tradition that has determined the destiny of every Eritrean girl. Eritrean women were supposed to get married and look after their husband and home at a very young age.

When I finished high school with good grades, I knew my time had come. I knew that Aboy could not shield me forever. But somewhere, mine and Aboy's resolve was so strong that it swayed even God to show his hands. God sent Eyob to answer all my prayers.

When Eyob came to ask for my hand in marriage, he told my family that he would leave for the USA soon after marriage. He had his dreams of getting a higher education and making something of his life. Aboy took him in confidence and told him all about our mutual dream.

Fortunately, my husband was cut out of the same cloth as Aboy. He had no qualms about women getting higher education. He agreed to the idea of taking me to the USA for further studies.

It was not that my family and I accepted Eyob because he was taking me abroad; he also had other very desirable qualities. He was a compassionate, committed, and very compatible young man. All these qualities and our mutual dream tied us in the matrimonial knot, and I would be eternally grateful to God for this fate.

While I was about to build a relationship with Eyob, the political climate was about to be get chaotic.

At home, my life was no less chaotic. It was going through significant alteration. My wedding date was fixed. Everything was settled, and wedding plans were in motion. My mother was enthusiastic about an Eritrean wedding. I was happy and excited to start my new life with Eyob. He was an ideal husband from every aspect.

However, life always brings unexpected things. Eyob had to leave soon after the wedding. Therefore, we had to make many changes to our plan. But despite all the alterations and chaos, my wedding ceremony was full of colors and delight.

For me, the city of Asmara shrank into wedding tailors and rental shops, where I had to rush to order my white wedding gown and other outfits like, Zurias, set of suites for honeymoon and jewelries to match the traditional white dresses.

When my wedding date came near, I was restricted to staying home by my mother, following the Eritrean tradition. But the bridesmaids were out and about to find the right traditional shoes, jewelry, and other accessories to go with the wedding dress.

Even with all the preparation, we still had to make a few adjustments where usually the bride will have to adjust it a few times. As the wedding day approaches, the bride fasts for five days, to lose weight, and be well fitted to her wedding outfits.

Then comes the family members, brothers, and sisters, who also have to ensure that their outfit is another task for the future bride and groom.

The same excitement and hustle bustle of a wedding home was going on at Eyob's place as well. He and his friends were exploring the marketplace to select the suits to go with the color theme we had decided. I paid extra attention to the color theme to align everything with the same hues, from the venue decoration to the invitation cards.

We followed all the traditions of an Eritrean wedding. *Suwa*, a traditional drink made of a mix of grains such as millet and sorghum; the making is long. It requires time and intense monitoring. At the same time the making it is so entertaining; women gather singing wedding songs and dance.

The beautiful chants of those women combined with traditional coffee to give some energy. *Mies*, another traditional booze made of fermented honey and very appreciated by young women for its sweet taste.

The bride, on her side, is often asked to remain at home and take care of herself starting a week before the wedding. It can be quite a difficult time for a control-freak bride.

At 4 am on Saturday, time for photos with family, and finally, the groom in his traditional white outfit accompanied by his best men and friends comes to take the bride towards the church.

A very early ceremony usually takes about two hours if it's an orthodox church. Thus, it requires patience—a wonderful choir of the church, where priests call in unison for the blessings of the newlyweds. The groom with his entourage will take the bride home. Then in the afternoon, with his entourage go to the bride's home. Then officially in a traditional way, the ceremony of a father giving away his daughter to her husband and exchanging introduction of family trees on both sides goes on (in the old days there was the dowry ceremony). They will thank one another the groom with entourage takes his bride home.

Over time, however, celebrations became more flexible. A few days later, the bride will braid her hair again and make a traditional hand and foot design with henna. She will wear a traditional dress. It is time for "*Hamawiti*." In other words, the bride's family, the women, in particular, will come to the groom's house to celebrate together and bring offerings to the groom's mother.

They will feast and complement one another (the in-laws) and the bride's mother will have a chance to coach up on the marital life. The in laws will be dancing to music, expressing their happiness together.

It might seem like a long process. However, the beauty of the tradition makes the stress and fatigue swiped out by the happiness of families. Many would forget that weddings are not just the union of two people but two families.

However, for me, fortunately, or unfortunately, my marriage had zoned into one objective only. I was more focused on continuing my studies than starting my married life.

I shifted to my in-law's house. A few months after our wedding, Eyob left for the United States of America., leaving me behind in Asmara to wait for the most desired call to come.

The days after Eyob were full of monotony. As a new bride, I did not have much household work to do. As a daughter-in-law of a traditional family, I hesitated to socialize in my friends' circle.

Waking up to a long day ahead took a toll on my mind. I counted days for my departure to join my husband in the US and join the broken connection of my education.

On the other hand, I watched my other friends find their exit in various ways. Some were applying for student exchange programs; others were spending money to attend foreign universities.

After all, everyone saw the trapped future that was rapidly taking hold of Eritrea. At the same time, the Eritrean struggle for independence grew tremendously; most youth, especially boys, left in abundance.

I was frustrated witnessing all that was happening in and around my beloved Asmara, watching all my friends leave one by one. At the same time, I was bound financially and traditionally in the country. Six months had passed. Each day was different from another. One day I was full of anticipation and excitement, while the next day, I was surrounded with gloom and hopelessness.

It was a bright day in Asmara when I finally got the call I had been waiting for. I was excited beyond words.

I forgot to reach my dreams in the excitement of getting near my ambition. I had to get my feet off the ground. I had to uproot myself from my lands. I will never forget the despair and heartbreak that I felt and witnessed on my family's face.

I left Asmara with excitement for the new beginning, enclosed in a heavy heart that was weeping to say farewell to the family and friends with whom I had spent my whole life. My roots were in Asmara, and it hurt to uproot myself from my homeland.

My first stop was in Italy, Europe, and another life experience for me. I missed my scheduled ride to the hotel; fortunately, this taxi driver realized I was lost, with my little broken Italian and sign language he took me to a small hotel owned by a family.

I stayed there with a family, which was a combination of the excitement of meeting new people and the anxiety of being with people who didn't even speak the language I knew. But my head was all over the place due to mixed feelings.

My time with the Italian family became more enjoyable when I found a guy who knew about Eritrea, my language. He said his great grand dad was in Asmara during the Italian colony. I sat beside him at dinner and talked about Asmara. His great grandfather was one of the owners of the Textile Company in Asmara. He knew a lot about Masawa, Nefasit and Dongolo, their vacation destinations during the Italian colony.

I needed someone to talk about what I had left behind. After taking to my new friend, I felt a bit lighter. The rest of my journey towards the United

States became easier for me. I had more energy and enthusiasm to focus on my future life in the US with my husband. Little did I know about my future? I set out to reach my destination and an unknown fate.

CHAPTER 04 | A NEW HOME

Splendid to arrive alone in a foreign country and feel the assault of difference. Here they are all along, busy with living; they don't talk or look like me. The rhythm of their day is entirely different; I am foreign.

– Frances Mayes

I arrived as a foreigner, an alien, a migrant, in America. It was a cold December dawn when I touched the land of dreams. America, as expected, was completely opposite of Asmara for me. The bustling crowd, giant skyscrapers, and a sense of urgency in the atmosphere instead of the serenity of Asmara.

I, wide-eyed Senbet, left the airport and stepped into the American streets with dreams of higher education and a progressive future.

It was Christmas time, and there was an air of festivities all around me. I have heard of the American Dream and have been preparing for it since my marriage to Eyob. Now, I ventured to find my own place in it.

My initial days and nights were immersed in the Christmas merriments. The huge cultural gap between Eritrea and America was overwhelming, making me confused and vulnerable. My arrival day

Eyob was out of town. I was greeted by the son of the landlady and his girlfriend

Needless to say, that everything was shockingly new for me. The way the couples dress, (it was the hippy style early seventieth). Most of the Anglo-Saxon couples, both boys and girls had their hair long to their waistline and wore a long overcoat. It was new to me.

Eyob was friends with the American couple. When we arrived at their house it was the time of Christmas Eve Celebration.

Our hosts invited us to freshen up and join the family for Christmas dinner. Honestly, I was not ready to mingle in any kind of socialization.

I was already, overwhelmed by the gap between Eritrean and American culture. Yet I came downstairs to witness the dinner celebration.

It was my first buffet-style dining, and the food was entirely different than my traditional spicy Berbere (especially made with more than ten herbs).

It was my first encounter with a dinner of pork, mashed potatoes, and Mac 'n' cheese. It was all new to me and made me crave for my traditional spicy hot pepper and *E*NGERA (traditional bread). I still managed to celebrate with the family who were so kind and inviting to me.

My next astonishing encounter was my first Thanksgiving in the USA. My husband, I and our friends were all newcomers.

Our friends decided to celebrate the occasion together. We gathered on Thanksgiving morning to go out to eat, only to find that everything was closed.

It was cold, and we did not know exactly how to dress up for the harsh cold winter, or where to find something to eat. We kept walking for almost half of the day and eventually stumbled upon Chinatown, open for business.

At last, we were able to feed ourselves. It was again something completely different from Asmara, where streets and bazaars were always scattered with more food stalls and roadside peddlers in festive seasons.

The market where the countryside people come to sell and city people to purchase. To witness the transaction and all. The aroma of traditional food in the air the bell sounds of churches and mosque was one of the signs that Eritreans were celebrating.

After these shocking experiences, I promised my friends that I would cook every Thanksgiving Day at my place, wherever it would be.

When we reached home, the question loomed bigger than ever in front of me: how I would survive in a foreign land, surrounded by new people since my experiences and exposure were very limited. The financial burden was unthinkable. Eventually, my hesitation led to decide that Eyob would start school, and I will wait and join him a semester later.

My transnational experience, from a student to bride and yet not fully realizing that being at home here is to study for my future's change and at same time to be a wife. It was a challenge. And that was what happening with me.

It was at this time that Eyob and his friends decided to take me to NY to show me around. The trip was both, exhilarating and fascinating for me at the same time. The fast-moving mass of people, the speedy cars on the wide and four Lanes Streets were new to me.

I have never seen as many taxi cabs in my life. And most shockingly amazing was to see the high-rise buildings, particularly Empire State Building! It was entirely a trilling voyage.

However, it is true that the necessity is the mother of invention. I realized that moving abroad is the mother of reinvention.

I understood in little time that one of the most profound facets of migrating to a new country is that life gives us an opportunity to reinvent ourselves in ways we never imagined possible.

I resolved that whether I fall on my face, I fail, but at least I would have the satisfaction of trying my level best. And if nothing works out, I will again stand up to reinvent myself.

CHAPTER 05 | STRUGGLES

When you move from one country to another you have to accept that there are some things that are better and some things that are worse, and there is nothing you can do about it.

— Bill Bryson

I was gradually beginning to assimilate into my life in the new country and home. It didn't take much time for me to realize that to start a full-fledged life as a student and a society member in America; I will have to overcome various challenges. Yet it was not easy.

One of the biggest challenges was the language barrier. Back in Eritrea, early education is thought in mother's language and the nine local languages were spoken at home, notably, in Asmara, we used to attend early education school in our mother tongue. Tigrinya and Arabic were mainly used in commerce and national business. The dominant foreign language was English.

Italian was another language that I thought would have been easier for me to grasp because thousands of Italians settled in Eritrea, mainly Asmara, by the end of the nineteenth century while Italian colonial rule till 1941. Therefore, many older Eritreans used to speak Italian, and we, the younger ones, have caught the gusts of the language, making it easier for us to understand and learn it.

English has become a language of instruction in secondary schools and the University of Asmara and is fast becoming the foreign language of choice. If it had been the scenario in my time in Asmara, I would not have faced the difficulty of learning the language.

Learning the traditional ropes was another hurdle that I had to cross. But when it came to traditions and culture, the problem was entirely different than learning the language. While learning the American vocabulary, I had to grasp the skills.

To get used to the traditions, I had to let go of many things that were embedded in my being. For example, greeting people or sitting at a discussion table with groups, here you have to look at people eye to eye to make sure that you're following them, and they follow you.

On the other hand, the tradition back, home is that it is very rude to look at a person eye to eye, especially elders. You are supposed to keep your head bowed while speaking to them. Even though I had some English learning back home, compared to the American English (the accent) it seemed like a different language to me and more, even the simplest matter of food was a challenge for me in America.

It wasn't easy to learn about the food. I was unaccustomed to cooking and eating such an abundance of baked food items. Meats and vegetables were supposed to be bought fresh from open markets, not refrigerated stores. At least, this is what the case was at that time. Cooking Eritrean food was not easy because it was not easy to find the ingredients. So, I had to learn American recipes that could be easy, yet I am determined to learn anything that I have to empower myself.

In fact, it would be more accurate to say that when I left home and tried to mingle in the society, I realized that the trend of discriminating against immigrants is very deep rooted in America. Even so, the country is mainly composed of immigrants and their descendants.

The harder I tried to get accepted, the harsher I was treated by the natives. Needless to say, my ignorance and lack of exposure benefited me not to pay attention any of them but to empower myself through education.

One would think that now when people have evolved with education and diverse cultural setting, racial discrimination has become a far-fetched idea. But it is evident through the recent events against black Americans that unfortunately, as time have gone by; the religious, cultural, and racial discrimination against immigrants has kept developing and become increasingly intense.

Even though Immigrants have made an enormous contribution to the United States, they have come to be regarded as outsiders who threaten the US political system and burden its finances and welfare. Immigrants used to be and will continue to be the victims of exclusion and persecution.

I can relate to the situation because I firsthand experienced the same. When I got out taking a job, even the humblest people treated me as an alien who had come to their country to rob them of their careers and positions, which were rightfully theirs. Some were subtle in making their point, but those who very aggressively showed that they would never accept me as part of their society.

Although, when I stepped out of the sanctuary of my home, it didn't take much time to find a suitable job.

The job was at a local grocery which was precisely what I was looking for, because with the lack of any skill and grasp of the language, this was all that I could handle at that time. But the realization that I was an outsider hit me hard on the face on the very first day of work.

The manager directed me to fill out an application form. Since it was the first time I was applying for a job, least of all in a strange country, the documentation immensely confused me—the documentation and information I was supposed to provide utterly boggled my mind. The manager offered to help.

During the process, the manager asked me to fill in if I was black or white, to which I said, "Neither! I am Eritrean." The manager eyed me critically, stating in a firm tone that it is in the application requirement, so I must choose the appropriate answer.

I asserted that this requirement must be for Americans, but it shouldn't apply to me since I am an Eritrean immigrant. The manager then suggested to find someone who could understand my native language and English to help me appropriately fill the form.

As confused as I was, I have to sick for help. As luck would have it, I had recently met an Ethiopian immigrant woman, Meseret, who had moved to the US years prior.

I had to be very diplomatic with Meseret's help to fill in the application. Meseret is Ethiopian and I am Eritrean, both belonging to the rival countries was an issue. Meseret believed that we are both Ethiopian. I had to explain that Eritrea has been colonized by Italians, British then annexed with Ethiopia by force.

It was the first memory of the difficulty that I faced due to the language and culture, barrier, but thanks to my friendly nature that has helped me find a good rapport with people around me; I eventually received my first job.

By then, the inability to quickly accept the American diet, the drastic cultural and environmental change, and the feeling of being alienated had drained my energy. I felt terribly homesick. I was beginning to lose weight.

At this point, my landlady, Ms. Smith, took me to a doctor for proper medical help. I would be eternally grateful for all the gestures made by my American friends that helped me get through those tough times, and finally, I got better.

My complaint was I don't have an appetite to eat? The Doctor said OKAY don't eat. For two months here are these tablets, take one every day and come back to see me (I bet you they were just vitamins). When I hope everyday passes, I get so hungry that I will fix myself some toast with spinach and spice it with some berbere I got from home.

The two months went by, I went to see the doctor and I was so worried; because he told me don't eat so I cheated. I ate. It was embracing to me not following the doctor's order. The doctor has to explain it to me; I was just home sick and lost appetite but will be okay. Thanks to Mrs. Smith it was a relief.

While I was struggling in America with new learning and recurring challenges, many things were changing back at home.

As mentioned above, the crisis began to occur while I was about to leave for America. But now, the emperor, Haile Selassie, is overthrown by the Junta Military Colonel Mengistu Hailemariam. The Military Junta was supported by the Russians, and they blocked all communications and relations with the USA.

The war between Ethiopia and Eritrea had escalated to a level, with people fleeing to neighboring countries, teenagers, and mothers killed on the streets of Asmara.

The situation added to my dilemma. On top of my struggle to settle in the new country, I lost all communication with my family back at home. Aboy, who always gave me the strength to move forward, was no longer in touch with me.

The unrest of my beloved home began to take its toll on me. My tuition payment from home was also discontinued. During this crisis, I reached out to Eritrean Students, who contacted each other and formed the Eritrean Students Group, now known as

Eritrean Students in North America, my second family, which gave me a strong feeling of belonging.

That was my first milestone in the journey from being just a student but a nationalist Eritrean. More to learn about my native land and how colonization disrupted its growth and development. I learned stability is key for whatever to plan in life and determined to get stronger and playthings one at a time.

CHAPTER 06 | LESSONS

We cannot direct the wind, but we can adjust the sails. –

Dolly Parton.

Like a sailor adjust the sails of a ship on unknown water, to go smoothly in according to the dimension of wind, I also had to make lot of adjustments to my Asmarina ways to adjust in American culture.

"Time flies" is not just a cliché. I acknowledged it as a fact for the first time in my life in America. I have not fully learned the ropes of American life, and two months passed in snaps of fingers.

The good thing was that the time had come when all my dreams were about to come true. It was time when I had to join college to continue my studies. Saying that I was excited will be an understatement.

I was elated, happy beyond the possibility of describing in words. I was in a strange country, among strangers, just to fulfill my dream of getting higher education.

When I was about to start the first day of my college, the first person that I remembered the most was Aboy.

I remembered how he went against everyone to encourage me to continue my studies. He arranged the marriage between Eyob and me and sent me away from his sight, only so I could study further.

I was fully aware of the sacrifices that my parents, especially my Aboy, have made to help me chase my dream of becoming a highly educated Eritrean.

Knowing the sacrifices and compromises that my parents and I have faced to reach here, I was intensely committed to giving my 100% to my studies. I intended to become the top student at my college.

Eyob was with me all along the way, guiding me and encouraging me, taking my complete loyalty and gratitude in return.

Our schedule was tight. I had to take my classes, continue the store job, study hard and look after the household chores. I didn't want Eyub's needs to be neglected since everything he was doing for me.

I started college and soon was prospering among my classmates. Eyob was helping me as much as he could, but he was himself new in the country and focused on his own studies.

However, my enthusiasm to gain knowledge didn't waiver even for a second. The Eritrean Student Association was close to each other, and the association played a big role in my life.

I took every support and help I could get from my teachers, peers, and the books I could read. The biggest challenge was the language barrier. But gradually, I managed to grasp it so I could read more and more to stay with my peers.

The sense of being alienated was still there, but I have somehow dampened the intensity with my enthusiasm to learn and be equal to my peers who can always turn to my colleagues at the Eritrean Student Association and, my good friend Amy for all her encouragement.

A year passed in getting settled in the new culture. However, the process never hindered my learning process. At the beginning of the second year, I was settled with the cultural shock of the initial year. However, there was more to come in my life.

I soon discovered that I was pregnant. Although, it was too early. We were still settling in our new life in America. We were extremely excited we are going to be Three. It was such overwhelming news.

The feeling of expecting motherhood was elating. We both were happy and making plans for our baby. However, my excitement was a bit different from Eyob's.

I have already begun to plan how I will navigate through a new lifestyle, with a baby to take care of along with my studies and other responsibilities.

Days passed, and my pregnancy became mature with each day, making it more and more difficult for me to keep a hold on everything going on in my life. While Eyob continued to work and was immersed in completing his own education, I was trying to figure out a way to continue my college, have the baby to take care, and look after the house, Eyob.

By then, I had made friends with many women who were migrants like me. And Amy, who is American, was one of them and very close to me. I admired her strong personality and determination. She kept me motivated and encouraged me with her discussions and actions.

She was the optimum of strength and motivation. I have seen her manage her strong dedication to her studies and her family ties. She was and is quite an aspiration to me.

My studying for college was now disrupted by my eagerness to learn about bringing up an infant with no experienced adult around me. Parental books could be seen with my course books. Life has dramatically changed. I didn't know whether this change would affect my dreams, or I would manage to nurture both my dreams and my family.

One thing I was sure this baby is God's gift for me and I said no matter what, I will take care. When my parent got the news of my pregnancy, they offered to help me raise my baby until my studied done but I humbly declaimed the offer believing it is solely my responsibility to raise my baby.

In all this period, I learned a great lesson. Nothing happens according to our plans. God has his own plans, and our intention is mere words written on paper that can be erased at any point in time.

It's God's will that remains engraved on the stone and can be changed only if almighty feels like doing it. I learned the lesson of faith that the best time we recognize the power of God is when our intentions break, and plans fail in front of God's own will.

With this new faith in God's will, I knew that whatever would happen was beyond our control, and we would have to accept it as our destiny. All these thoughts.

Amy's motivation, Aboy's strong and spiritual inspiration and all the friends I acquire in time, gave me full strength to tackle my life.

There was a possibility that I would not be able to do it all at once, but I hoped that sooner or later, I would gain everything in life. But again, our plans, intentions, and predictions are nothing in front of what God wants for us.

The path that he chooses for us is the right one, and we have to walk it, no matter if we are unable to grasp the wisdom behind it.

A lot was about to change and happen in my life. But with so many life lessons and experiences, I was prepared to accept whatever may come my way, even in the strange country and among strangers where I could not communicate with my family as much as I wanted.

CHAPTER 07 | CHAOS IN ASMARA

Most gun control arguments miss the point. If all control boils fundamentally to force, how can one resist aggression without equal force? How can a truly "free" state exist if the individual citizen is enslaved to the forceful will of individual or organized aggressors? It cannot.

Tiffany Madison-

The Eritrean Revolution was overwhelming the military junta by capturing Villages, and Eritreans Nationals from all over the world were joining the Revolution.

And the situation back home was engulfed and the war effects in the City of Asmara were taking its toll. Parents of teenagers and adult kids were strained, not knowing what to do to protect their children.

At the beginning of 1970s, Ethiopia entered into profound economic, political, and social turmoil. The dilemma was that the period was frequently tinted by violence.

Frequent confrontations between modern and traditional forces erupted to disrupt the harmony of cities like Asmara.

In the last fourteen years of Haile Silesia's rule, the Ethiopian opposition grew to its peak. Although the emperor suppressed the 1960 coup attempt, he had to seek loyalty from coup sympathizers by setting up reform. Selassie granted substantial lands to police and military officers. However, the effort did not bring fruitful results as the emperor expected.

The question of Eritrean Independence and Ethiopian acceptance of Eritreans for independence was not resolved. There was no social and economic development against the reform.

The tension was building up in the country. The government could not bring any economic and political reform in the last fourteen years.

This, combined with elevating corruption, inflation, corruption, a famine that deteriorated the living conditions in several provinces, fueled the worsening political and economic conditions of Ethiopia.

If seen from an unbiased viewpoint, the decisions taken by the emperor also did not help his reign. For instance, the famine was deliberately concealed from the outer world, and the growing discontent of urban interest groups provided the backdrop against which the Ethiopian revolution began to unfold in early 1970s.

Whereas elements of the urban-based, modernizing elite previously had sought to establish a parliamentary democracy, the initiation of the revolution was the work of the military, acting essentially in its own immediate interests.

The unrest that began in January of that year then spread to the civilian population in an outburst of general discontent.

In late June, a body of men that eventually totaled about 120, none above the rank of major and almost all of whom remained anonymous, organized themselves into a new body called the Coordinating Committee of the Armed Forces, Police, and Territorial Army that soon came to be called the Derg (Amharic for "committee" or "council").

The group elected Major Mengistu Haile Mariam chairman and Major Atnafu Abate vice-chairman, both outspoken proponents of far-reaching change.

This group of men would remain at the forefront of political and military affairs in Ethiopia for the next thirteen years. However, the identity of the Derg never changed after these initial meetings in 1974.

Although its membership declined dramatically during the next few years as individual officers were eliminated, no new members were admitted into its ranks. Its deliberations and membership remained almost entirely unknown.

At first, the Derg's officers exercised their influence behind the scenes; only later, during the provisional

Military Administrative Council era, did its leaders emerge from anonymity and become both the official and the de facto governing personnel.

By late 1976, the Derg had undergone an internal reconfiguration as Mengistu's power came under growing opposition and as Mengistu, Tafari, and Atnafu struggled for supremacy.

The instability of this arrangement was resolved in January and February of 1977 when a major shootout at the Grand (Menelik's) Palace in Addis Ababa took place between supporters of Tafari and those of Mengistu in which the latter emerged victoriously.

With the death of Tafari and his supporters in the fighting, most internal opposition within the Derg had been eliminated, and Mengistu proceeded with a reorganization of the Derg.

This action left Mengistu as the sole vice chairman, responsible for the People's Militia, the urban defense squads, and the modernization of the armed forces. Whereas urban-based elements, modernizing elite in the past had sought to develop a parliamentary democracy. It was the beginning of the revolution by the military, who was basically acting in its own interests.

The turbulence started that year spread and reached the civilian population and resulted into an outburst of widespread discontent.

In the end of June, around 120 men, all under the rank of major. All those men remain anonymous till date. The small force established themselves into an organization called the Coordinating Committee of the Armed Forces, Police, and Territorial Army. They soon became known as the Derg (Amharic word for council or committee).

The Derg elected Major Mengistu Haile Mariam as a chairman and Atnafu Abate as a vice-chairman. Both these men were outspoken advocates of extensive change.

These men stabilized themselves at the forefront of military and political affairs in Ethiopia for thirteen years. However, their identity never changed after the preliminary meetings held in 1974, even when its membership dramatically declined in few years.

Individual officers were removed, without replacement of new members to fill the ranks. Its membership and deliberations remained completely unknown. Initially, the officers of this group practiced their effect behind the scenes. Later, in the era of provisional Military Administrative Council, its leaders emerged from obscurity and became both the de facto and official governing personnel.

By the end of 1976, the Derg reconfigured themselves internally as Mengistu's power went under increasing opposition and as Tafari, Mengistu, and Atnafu struggled for power.

The instable arrangement was however resolved in the beginning of 1977 after a shootout between Tafari's and Mengistu's supporters at Menelik's Grand Palace in Addis Ababa in which the Mengistu emerged as winner.

On the other hand, the Eritrean Armed Struggle was consolidating and becoming a united front, Eritrean People's Front.

With Tafari's death and his supporters' defeat in the fight, most of the internal antagonism within the Derg got eliminated. Mengistu, who became the only vice chairman reorganized the Derg. He also became responsible for People's Militia and the upgrading of the armed forces.

In other words, effective control of Ethiopia's government and military. Finally, in November 1977, Atnafu, Mengistu's last rival in the Derg, was eliminated, leaving Mengistu in undisputed command.

When these developments were taking place, I had already left for the USA. However, the effects of this political turmoil were already leaving their mark in the early 1970s.

As a part of the society obviously I would directly be affected. The worries, how my father is doing and not having the chance to guarantee the safety of the family became my concern.

With all the commotion going on, I delivered my son. We named him Tesfay, which means Our Hope. But my husband felt obliged to join the Eritrean Armed struggle, so he left a few months after the birth of our son. Needless to say, how hard is it to be a new mother with no mentors nearby?

At that time, my status in the US was of alien which is an Illegal Immigrant. I could not ask for help from any social services or government institution. If at all found by a USA Immigration service agent, I could have been deported.

The job opportunities were limited. As a new mother, in a strange culture not knowing how to navigate was hard. But, thanks to my colleagues, Eritrean students. I am particularly grateful to my friend Amy who often checked on me and my son. I started to work for a few hours a day only to cover for formula and baby food, not enough to cover my expenses.

My friend Asmait and her husband Asmerom are my childhood friends, and we would discuss my situation constantly. At one point, she invited me until I got situated and she was out of state.

They sent me a ticket to fly and soon I joined them. The three of us took turns to look after my baby and work. I was able to acquire some money for rent and deposit and come back to my town. Soon got an apartment and lob. I was settled and able to care for my son and me.

On the other hand, the situation in Eritrea got worse and the worries of my father and my siblings were unbearable. And planned to see how I can help. Would consult my friend Amy. She came up with an idea on how to get my sisters with student visa. The barrier is high expenses. While taking care of my child to fund my sibling's arrivals. She gladly confirms that she will help me if I need her to sponsor any of my siblings. With that information, I need money for plane tickets. I decide to work extra hours a day to save some money at the same time I would consult Amy about my plans.

Amy my life saver, she said "if the sponsor ship went well, I will finance your money that will be paid monthly or however you want so you can take care of you other expenses." Her motivation was a base to my ambition to the road in helping my siblings.

Imagine I am still Illegal immigrant working illegally and all the above. "If there is a will there's a way." I successfully brought two of my siblings and my heartfelt full and happiness.

It didn't take them long they would find any job, to full fill their daily needs and find ways to continue their education. Life was hard and easy if you all compromise and shoot for the best to come. We were all illegal immigrants.

We stayed in small apartment, even if we wanted, we couldn't rent a better place because of our status. We had to find a charity person to sponsor for the rental lease. With all our hardships we managed to move forward with our effort to live our life harmoniously.

Soon after I felt the urgency to see my parents and decide to try have them to visit.

It took a lot of time and effort to arrange the money, through work and loans. Finally, with the help from Amy and the funding I have gathered, I was able to arrange for my parents to visit. At long last, it happened it was the most memorable and blissful time I had. The happiness' of our union at the time is cherished for life.

Life and urgency are inseparable! Soon enough my worry for my other siblings follows. As usual with Amy's encouragement and support I overcome the financial burden and reunited with the other set of my siblings.

I was so overwhelmed by the reunion of my siblings peacefully with no incidents that I began to count my blessings.

The blessing kept on coming had my second son named him TeAmrat means a miracle, indeed it is.

This was a period people fleeing country by crossing the border, which claims so many lives of women and children. Lot was missing without a trace.

One of the stories is of our neighbor Aboy Mebrahtu went through. It was year 1978 when Dehab and Nebiat Aboy Mebrahtu's daughters decided to flee secretly from anyone. Their destination was Khartoum a city of Sudan. Voyage is by foot.

Dehab and Nebiat had no clue whatsoever, of what is waiting for them on the road or deed they understood the distance from their home Asmara to Khartoum was. They were just two underage girls trying to escape the horror of war happening in their town.

The first stop was to flee Asmara a city with a strong hold of military check points. The only qualified to travel through are the countryside people who come to the city to do their earrings and sell their farm products to the city consumers. So, Dehab and Nebiat have to work on their appearance as county women. Mostly they will pair with older country people pretending as young helpers. This process continues to find a village could be easy to cross the border.

Dehab and Nebiat assumption and expectation was way different than what was crossing the border took weeks and weeks. The hard ship, heat of the dessert, the dryness and thirst combined of days to walk became unbearable. Dehab got dehydrated and very sick. Dehab passed away before they cross the border. Poor Nebiat at a tender age she has to go through this tragic experience. Because, of the dessert's nature, the monsoon, dessert scorpions' bite and luck of drinking water all made hard for Nebiat to have a normal grieving time of her sister.

Nebiat had to reorganize and pull her thoughts together. Soon she began the voyage to cross the border. Her Agony seems never ending. Nebiat got caught by the traffickers on border before entering Sudan and arrested and bitten and blind folded tithed up, she had no clue of where they are taking her. Nebiat find here self at abandoned and half ruined place in a room by herself and all the bitten and relentless abuse stopped, but she has no clue what to do with that brief break she has. Survival!!! Nebiat decided to run away wherever her feet leads her. Again destiny! She landed in a middle of a city that boarder to capital city of Sudan. Disoriented and exhausted Nebiat wandered the streets.

Luck has it. This gentleman approaches Nebiat and asks her 'Gual Asmara!' means are you from Asmara. Nebiat felt haven opening up! After the whole ordeal of abuse and threat on her life to hear somebody speaking her language Tigrigna? She was num. The gentleman took her to his place and offered her to stay as long as she needed. For the first time through ordeal of almost half of a year, she has been Nebiat felt safe and fell asleep.

The gentleman offered Nebiat all the need, to stay, her room and food and any necessity. He advised her not to wonder around alone ' the traffickers are out there praying on newcomers like you if you have a plan to refuge and transfer overseas to the First World I can help you, but take your time and let me know'. Nebiat was so overwhelmed by the gesture and yet hesitant because of what she went through.

After one month of rest Nebiat decide to continue to refuge and to trust the generous gentleman to share her plan. He told Nebiat to register as a refuge and has to stay at refugee camp where to apply for refugee status. Nebiat, from previous experience she is confused if she should believe him or not but realized no other option.

Nebiat who have never been away from her mom and dad, siblings away, but within six month time she went through a whole deal of adventure, she decided to trust this gentleman and asked his name, he replied Abraham!

Abraham is an Eritrean refuge who settled in Sudan is store owner in the city and is well acquainted and knowledgeable of the system. Luckily, he was the best candidate to help Nebiat she was in good hands.

Nebiat began her process to acclaim a refugee status and had to move in at the Refugee Camp on the outskirt of the city Khurtum. Fortunately, she was well oriented and informed by Abraham for any incase or mishap he gave her his phone number so she could call him from anywhere. Abraham is Nebiat's Angel.

After six months stay at a refugee camp, with the help of Abraham Nebiat gets the approval of her refugee status. Followed she would be qualified to apply at one of the non-profitable organizations for refugee, eight months later she found a catholic charity to sponsor for the USA.

Two years since she left home Nebiat made it to land the soil of America and started to live her destinies. To live and learn a new culture and share all journey of Diasporas.

I Senbet feel am most blessed to have union of my siblings without the incidents, lot of Eritreans like Nebiat went and to have the chance to see my parents am most blessing.

Soon enough The Reagan Presidency offers a political amnesty for emigrants entered USA after 70th and automatically me and my siblings are qualified and are legally accepted to apply for residency.

It was a miracle after all the fear of deportation and not knowing of what to plan next! my sisters got permit to work and continue their education legally! It was indeed a relief.

The war of independence took root in Eritrea during the 1960s. The battle was led by the ELF (Eritrean Liberation Front). Initially, the military liberation movement started at the lowlands of Eritrea.

As the opposition escalated, the Ethiopian government began to play a game of divide and rule by trying to create a division among the Highlanders and Lowland of Eritrea, playing the religion card and ethnicity to serve their brutal purpose. The military aggression gotten more extensively intense towards the lowlands.

Despite, the Eritrean people Muslim Christian, lowlander highlander together, they prayed and protected one another more united than ever. Their theme was 'Eritrea Never Neal's'.

The war began in the literal sense on September 1, 1961, when Hamid Idris Awate and his companions fired the first shots against the occupying Ethiopian army and police.

The Emperor Haile Selassie of Ethiopia unilaterally dissolved the Eritrean parliament in 1962 and annexed Eritrea with Ethiopia. The propaganda of dividing Eritrea through religion, ethnic, and national difference among Eritreans by Colonizers coast resulted into a civil war.

With all the obstacles from external and internal enemies, the People of Eritrean got their dream Independence!! On May 24/1991

Although the United States refrained from intervening in the cold war between the Ethiopian army and EPLF. Later, for some reason, it entered into the peace talks to end the war.

May 24 1991 is a historic and most memorable day for every Eritrean. Eritreans from all over the world, celebrated for days and weeks. Even children born at a Diasporas overwhelmingly celebrated. It was the Momentums! Highest equilibrium of happiness of Mass Celebration for Eritreans all over the world.

There was a spirit of celebration among Eritreans everywhere. People started inquiring for lights to go visit home. The chant was Home! Sweet home!

During the Derg era any communication in or out of Eritrea was blocked. There were no commercial flights, both local and international and no phone connection. The situation made it difficult to travel to Eritrea from anywhere immediately after May 24/1991.

The first flight to depart from USA was Air India and the destination was only from NY. This didn't stop anyone's desire to go home and visit.

Like any Eritrean in USA, I tried to reserve and catch a flight home. After a long six months wait for flight reservation, I got lucky and traveled to NY for departure to Asmara. My reservation was for the month of December, Christmas season.

It was a déjà vu sensation. My mind was repeatedly flashing back to my Christmas arrival in America. My feeling was all mixed up. The excitement to see my ancestors land was mixed with the anxiety to acknowledge that who survived the war and who did not?

Even though I knew the passing away of my father previously, it all started to feel fresh and I couldn't separate it from past. I started grieving all over again;

it reminded me all of my father's wishes for his family and what the family went through during the war! How they handled and how they are affected by my father's loss? With all the fear and anxiety, the day of December 1991 came, when I landed in Asmara.

Seeing a war torn Asmara, I literary cried all the way from the airport to my parent's house. The rage of war destruction left my beautiful city Asmara marked with agony and grief!

CHAPTER 08 | FAMILY

Family means nobody gets left behind or forgotten

-David Ogden Stiers

In all my time, I have not forgotten my family even once. But this was the most crucial time because I was receiving alarming news from Asmara. I started receiving calls from my family. I, craving to talk to my family, had no idea that I would be reconnected to my family in this way with such drastic news.

Your family members are ones who always have your back in times need when you need support. And my family was the perfect example of such support system. They cheered for me on my successes; and laughed with me during my silliest slip-ups.

We were a clan, a network, a tribe, a true essence of family. Whatever you name it, they were always there when I needed them, even when not physically, they were there to morally support me in my direst times.

However, this time they needed me. Amidst a tense political climate, my family's business and all the assets they owned were confiscated by the Military Junta.

Government officials depicted by Mengistu in Addis Ababa were constantly introducing unreasonably strict laws, banning Eritrean political parties. They have stopped Eritreans from collecting their rightful portions of tax earnings and customs. Even Eritrean newspapers were censored, banned from writing the actual situation and spreading awareness.

The early years of the Selassie regime resulted in significant developments in Asmara, like the construction of mosques, churches, and hospitals, where people could freely practice their religion and address their basic health needs.

However, a lack of investment in later years, combined with a downfall in industrial activities, resulted in the stagnation of urban development in the city. The few industries settled by the British were dismantled and shifted to Addis Ababa. The shift ensured that the economic capability of the country was undermined.

In 1959, native languages Arabic and Tigrinya were already forbidden as instructional languages in educational institutions, and Amharic was introduced in its place. This has caused a barrier for many Eritreans in making progress in their academic fields.

Student boycotts and protests conducted by the labor class and civil officials were brutally answered by the Ethiopian police, leading to extreme violence. A general strike in 1958 left many dead and injured, and in other protests, Eritreans were arrested or forced into exile. Appeals to the United Nations were ignored.

The change of the road names in Asmara also had a significant impact on the city's identity. Today, the central Corso Italia Harnet Avenue, which was still called Viale Benito Mussolini before the British occupation, was renamed Haile Selassie I Boulevard.

Almost all of Asmara's street names were changed during the Ethiopian occupation to repress the memory of the Italian past and establish Ethiopian authority regarding the city's identity.

May 1991 was the historic month in Eritrean history, which marked the victory in the three-decades-long war of independence. However, the sacrifices that the ordinary people of Eritrea faced in this war can make up a bible reflecting the consequences of political instability in a country.

The EPLF attacked the Derg regime in Keren and Dekemhare, which were liberated recently in July 1977. By the end of the 1970s, most Eritrean towns were finally in control of Eritrean liberals. Nakfa was one of them.

So were the towns of Digsa and Segeneyti, who got their independence in July 1977. Among these towns, Keren held the most importance and had strengthened the Front where weaponries and artillery were ceased to bolster the Front's capacity.

In this era and onwards, the youth left in Eritrea escaped the Derg regime and joined the armed struggles seeing the consecutive conquests of the Front. The liberation struggle was conducted mainly through the town of Keren. Many students had already left for developed countries' incapacity of education-based immigrations in the early 1970s.

At that time, the story of a young woman Zewdi became quite popular among Eritreans living in and outside of Eritrea.

The story touched my heart too, and I still remember the details told to me by my parents in one of the letters or phone calls. I don't know the source exactly. However, the incident is still fresh in my mind as if it happened just a day before.

Zawadi decided to join the war of independence at the tender age of thirteen. She planned to keep her parents and siblings in the dark because she knew they would never let her participate in any dangerous movement, regardless of purpose.

Although she was too young, this adorable young girl with curly hair and deep eyes wanted to contribute by joining hands with her brothers, who were keeping their lives in line with the revolutionary movement.

Like every young woman living in Asmara, Zewdi had everything from a carefree life to a beautiful environment to breathe in. Her family was among the well-off families of the city, yet she always thought that something was amiss in her life.

She could not find peace due to the constant fear that the Derg would kill her and his family any day. Each time she left the house, it was with a fear that she wouldn't be able to see her siblings on her return, who had already joined the armed struggle with the cause of liberating Eritrea.

Her older sister, Ghenet, an activist and student in Asmara, somehow found out that her younger sister had left for the city of Keren. Along with her aunt, she embarked on a journey to look for her.

One morning, they boarded a bus that had to pass through many small towns near Asmara. When the bus was heading towards Himbirti, another small town, it had to stop at a checkpoint controlled by the Derg regime. The Derg people ordered everyone out of the bus and told them to sit on the ground in a queue.

The sun was hitting Ghenet's beautiful long hair when a soldier called her, the aunt discreetly following her chanting the words "nezamerat gualey intay delikhuma" (what do you want with my newly married daughter). The young girl was kept captured and interrogated the entire day.

Everyone witnessed her confidence even though she was scared for her, and her sister's lives but refused to show any outward sign of fear.

During that time, EPLF had already conquered the town of Keren. Therefore, any movement in that direction would be suspicious for the Dergs. Ghenet repeatedly told them that she was going to the nearby village with her aunt, till the soldiers decided to free the passengers.

Ghenet and her aunt continued their journey towards Keren, keeping only one thing in mind that they must find Zewdi. The incident further shook them, and they were terrified of the 13-year-old girl.

Finally, Ghenet and her aunt approached Keren, and again, they were stopped by another checkpoint… but this time, by Tegadelti, EPLF fighters.

Furthermore, long hours of interrogation to Ghenet ensured that she was one of them. Finally, they embarked on another bus and an EPLF bus. The music is on. Everyone is singing and dancing on the bus under the hit revolutionary songs of the EPLF, such as Woino! Woinona!!!

Ghenet could see a glimpse of Keren, reaching the liberated zone at last. Upon arrival, Ghenet and her aunt walked around the famous roundabout of the center of Keren.

A slight silhouette wearing the beige uniform of Tegadelti with afro curly hair appeared in the middle of the crowd.

It was Zewdi, the Asmarino teenager who is now an EPLF fighter… Ghenet ran towards her and greeted her little sister with hugs, cries, and cries. Zewdi looked different in her military outfit, her afro hair but holding the same beauty as her older sister.

After extended greetings, the siblings and aunt sat down to have tea in the Tegadelti's compound. Zewdi wanted to stir the sugar in her tea, but she could not find a spoon. As a habit, she took out a pen from her pocket and just used it as a teaspoon.

Ghenet looked at her in surprise, thinking of what her younger sister had back in Asmara, and now, she is already carrying the spirit of the fighters. Jokes, talks, stories continued in the little shelter, and Zewdi suddenly said: "sine sirat gerkum tezarebu, bebetera tezarebu" telling her elders to talk one by one and with discipline.

All astonished looked at her. The EPLF School has already taught her the importance of discipline. The little Asmara girl is now a grown-up and conscious young woman who has learned the principles of the EPLF: discipline, consciousness, commitment, self-reliance, camaraderie.

Ghenet, as a responsible older sister, tried to convince Zewdi to return home with her, at least until she got older. But Ghenet realized how the little girl in her teens was already consciously strong and eager to follow what she believed was the right decision, in other words, to fight for the rights to self-determination and liberation of the people of Eritrea.

When Zewdi joined the EPLF in the late 70s, women already had taken important roles as equal to their male counterparts during the armed struggle, thus, challenging the cultural doctrines of the patriarchal Eritrean society.

Zewdi, then, went back to her compound with her other comrades. As the situation started to tilt in favor of the enemy again with new attacks from Ethiopia and its new ally, the Soviet, Ghenet and her aunt quickly returned to Asmara.

The late 1970s showed a new shift in the struggle for independence since the first EPLF Congress of January 1977 in the Sahel and the adoption of a program to create an independent, secular and independent state.

Besides this, the program also focused on the liberalization of women's rights, particularly regarding access to land and property, and an education policy in all languages to fight illiteracy.

Liberating the town of Keren also coincides with the first congress and establishment of the National Association of Eritrean Youth and Students held in the symbolic city of Keren in 1978. It also marks the birth of National Union of Eritrean Women.

This is one of the many stories that occurred in between the political chaos in Eritrea. Families were scattered and children lost their homes. There was war everywhere.

May 24, 1991 The answer of every Eritrean prayer!

Like the Eternal light at Arlington Cemetery for the late president John F Kennedy. The Eternal light lit by our Great grandfathers Aboy Ibrahim Kebire and Aboy Woldeab Woldemariam glorified on our Independence Day May 24, 1991.

It started the late 50th with a song by the legend AteweBrhan Segid Adeye Adi Geganu means my country a country of braves. And now at the 22nd century our youth is enjoying the freedom and sense of belonging. Tewelide1 Nadeye! Tewelide, Anes Nadeye Nrime! Means, born for my country my pelage for my country.

CHAPTER 09 | REUNION

The strength of a family, like the strength of an army, lies in its loyalty to each other.

– Mario Puzo

It makes me sleep peacefully because I was loyal to them and vice versa when the time needed it most. Our loyalty, love, and consideration kept us knitted as a family even when were seas apart in distance and there were endless hurdles keeping us reaching to each other.

After my first visit of Eritrea I felt the urge and responsibility to show my children their native land and people soon enough managed to take and show my children the mother land. The most full feeling and cherished time was my children spending time with my mother.

Eritrea becomes a Mecca for Eritreans @ Diaspora. Every year summer Diaspora children flew to Eritrea and there the Festival Expo in Asmara is center of attraction for the young Diaspora. It is one of the mingling places for local and Diaspora youth.

Despite all that occurs. The Eritrean people at home or Diasporas are determined to keep the peace and harmony of the country.

Eritreans travel homeland for Wedding, Independence Day ceremony Summer Festival and many other occasions. The enthusiasm of homeland grows by minute.

CHAPTER 10 | MEMORIES

Winter is the time for comfort, for good food and warmth, for the touch of a friendly hand and for a talk beside the fire: it is the time for home.

– Edith Sitwell.

My fate chose a winter season for me to return home, the perfect time to revisit the childhood memories.

The year 1991 is marked by the independence of Asmara. But it took another ten years for the city to restore its glory.

I was ultimately settled in the U.S., my kids grown and intelligent enough to understand things by then. It was time to revisit the past, Asmara, my beloved hometown. There was no barrier between me and my childhood home. I could visit it anytime. However, the U. S was the home base for my children, and I could never think of uprooting my children for any of my selfish reasons.

The radical architecture of Italy tells its own tale of the Italian hold on the city. Mussolini prompted Italian engineers and architects to make Asmara into a municipal utopia.

The high number of cinemas, cafés, sycamore trees, and imported bicycles result from the same transformation.

After independence, Asmarian architecture was once again revealed to the world, open for everyone to explore. So, I explored them too, with my kids, as a family, as Asmarians. And each trip to the red sea beaches, cinemas, and museums was filled with talking about Asmara and its history and my childhood in the beautiful town.

I tried to transfer whatever knowledge I had about the city and poured whatever I knew about my city into my children's minds. The ruling of Egyptians, the Italians, the British, and then the Ethiopians.

The three decades of conflict with Haile Selassie's Ethiopian army and the brave people of Asmara and Eritrea who fought in the face of all this to eventually win its independence in 1991. I wanted my children to feel the connection that I felt with Asmara.

I knew I would never take away my children from the place they call home, but I wanted them to feel that deep down, my roots and their roots relate to Asmara. According to U.N. sanctions, Eritrea is a rugged country to enter as a tourist or journalist.

However, the large diaspora can visit their hometowns frequently thanks to the authorities. So, taking advantage of the liberty, I frequently visited Asmara with my family. Whenever I entered Asmara, an immense feeling of pride filled my chest, bursting.

I am proud of Asmara's resilience against time and crisis. No matter, the political history and the invasions have been brutal to the Asmarian citizens, but amazingly and strangely, the time has been kind to its architecture. All the conflicts that revolve around the city have encased Asmara's architecture into a time capsule. The art deco at cinemas, bowling alleys sporting antique wooden pins, cycling boulevards, and pizzerias are preserved like jewels in the Asmarian crown.

When Eritrea gained its independence on May24, 1991, I finally had a chance to go home and visit after 18 years. My first visit to Eritrea was extremely emotional because the loss of my dad hit me with full force when I entered home.

But at the same time, there were good memories too. The memories of my childhood and adolescent days were fresher when I was in my hometown.

As soon as I got to my childhood home, I was welcomed by warm kisses and hugs from my mom. Soon after settling down, I started having visitors from all over my aunts, cousins and relatives. My mother and everyone else would ask about my children and my siblings.

It was soothingly familiar to sit with life-long relative and friends, catching up on our homes and lives. We talked about the glorious days of school.

I immensely felt that how my life had been moving on an accelerated route since then, not always going towards the best direction. I absorbed a feeling of well-being from friends who married their childhood sweethearts, setting up homes only a stone throws away from where we grew up. They were the ones who were keeping the heartbeat of Asmara beating rhythmically.

I remember the night in one of my visits. My children had slept, and I was restless. We had a return flight for the U.S. the next day. So, I decided to take a walk around my childhood home.

Walking along the city's streets on a fantastic, dark August evening brought memories, but it also hit me how much Asmara has changed. The darkness was bleak around me due to the electricity shutdown announced by the government every evening. I could feel the city's stillness, narrating the tragedies it went through.

I could feel the Asmara bleeding in memory of all the citizens who had to leave the shelter of their city and go out into the cruel world instead to seek refuge and protection from outsiders. The good thing was that the streets were busy, but Alien armies harassed the leftover people of Asmara without the clatter.

It was not winter but the aura around me made me remember something I read somewhere, winter in hometown is comfort, warmth, touch of a friendly hand, and discussions around the fire.

After living in the hustle-bustle of American cities, I was glad to appreciate the Asmara with gusto. The difference between chaos and cool was evident in front of me. At night, the cafés were complete. I could see from across the glass panes of the vicinity. But there was a kind of serenity. No one was in an unknown hurry.

I took a cab in a desire to see Harnet Avenue, previously known as Mussolini Avenue and Haile Selassie Avenue. The names were a painful reminder of the city's endurance, the racial segregation Asmara had to go through when Eritreans were not allowed to enter this street.

Those who entered deliberately or unknowingly were arrested, imprisoned by Ethiopian soldiers, and had to go through the worst scenario consequences. Now, on this date, Eritreans are everywhere on Harnet Avenue, moving freely around doing their things. However, those who know the past can feel a cloud of repression hanging over the city.

Soon after I came back, I wanted to have my children visit my homeland and see their grandmother who was so anxious to see them. It took some time for my kids to understand and feel the essence of Asmara. Scratch the surface.

You will find the history of Asmara, rich in culture and traditions. And that is what gives an enigmatic beauty to the city.

Efforts are being made to preserve the city, but the process has always been gradual, perhaps due to Eritrea's still shaky economic conditions. Those loyal to Asmara have put great effort into declaring Asmara as a UNESCO World Heritage site.

I would heartily vote for the deed because the city's heritage and history can be keenly felt on the streets. The Italian influence lingers. Vintage Beetles and Volkswagen are still seen stuttering down the wide streets. You will see bicycles everywhere, making the road a historic sight to behold.

I was always in love with my hometown, but now more than ever before, I have come to love the resilience of my city.

Even after all the economic and political hardships, the brave face it put forth. In the hands of all the

Asmarians, US Diasporas, and our children to keep the history fresh for the world, telling the tale of bravery that the city and its residents showed in the face of crisis.

The time-wrapped art deco, emerging from all the challenges, gives a sense of pride to its past and present residents, and I hope that it will continue to do so in the future.

Visiting the countryside, the beaches of the Red Sea, and recounting the tales of Asmara, where I grew up with all my memories, I wish that my dreams were different. Or perhaps my dreams could be fulfilled in Asmara.

Sometimes I want to. I could have been here when people like Ghenet and Zawadi were putting their brave faces to fight for Eritrea. But then I look at my children and their faces and think that God has a will, and everything that happens, happens for a reason.

Still, I can't stop myself from wondering if all my dreams are worth leaving my hometown.

Of course, if someone can read my thoughts, they would look at me and say, 'What you are talking about, Senbet? You have had a life here for so long. You went to college here, however, for a short span. You gave birth to children here, and you are still not grateful. Yes, on the surface, I belong here now, but a soul never leaves home.

A home is one that always remains familiar, a home is one space in the world that belongs to you, and you belong to it. Home is where you stand in the window and stare into the night sky to let go of all the worries and negativities in the world. And yes, I have that home in America too.

However, my soul still longs for the streets of Asmara, for the courtyard of our house, for the room that was my sanctuary, and for the rising aroma of Zignis that was my mother's specialty. Even though now I am a full-fledged U.S. citizen, my heart and soul will always belong to Asmara. I am not being ungrateful. I am being a refugee. I am being an Asmarian.

Made in the USA
Monee, IL
08 December 2024